S0-BYJ-196

GONE FISHING

BRIAN GAUVIN

PHOTO: MARK HOBSON

Sono
Nis
Press

VICTORIA, BRITISH COLUMBIA / 1995

GONE FISHING
BRIAN GAUVIN

WITH A FOREWORD BY ALAN HAIG-BROWN

Copyright © 1995 Brian Gauvin

ALL RIGHTS RESERVED

Canadian Cataloguing in Publication Data

Gauvin, Brian, 1946-
  Gone fishing

ISBN 1-55039-060-0

  1. Fisheries—British Columbia-Pictorial works. 2.
Fisheries—British Columbia—Poetry. I. Title.
SH224.B7G38 1995   639.2'09711   C95-910532-8

This book was published with the assistance of
The Canada Council Block Grant Programme.

Published by
SONO NIS PRESS
1725 Blanshard Street
Victoria, British Columbia
Canada V8W 2J8

Designed, printed and bound by
MORRISS PRINTING COMPANY LTD.
Victoria, British Columbia

To Gail Blayney ❧

There are things out there in the depths which no man's nets have ever touched, and I shall bring them bright and struggling into the light. I shall find them.

J. MICHAEL YATES

Contents

The Poets

The poetic images accompanying Brian Gauvin's visual images were selected by Ann J. West. They were chosen from over 85 books of poetry published under the Sono Nis Press imprint since 1968. Only two excerpts are outside the SNP list.

GEORGE AMABILE   MARILYN BOWERING   BRIAN BRETT

ROBERT BRINGHURST   GWLADYS DOWNES   MARNIE DUFF

HAROLD ENRICO   RALPH GUSTAFSON   JAMES HARRISON

THERESA KISHKAN   ZOË LANDALE   CHARLES LILLARD

DOROTHY LIVESAY   SUSAN MUSGRAVE   RONA MURRAY

HAROLD RHENISCH   ROBIN SKELTON   SÉAN VIRGO

J. MICHAEL YATES   ANN YORK

Acknowledgements

I would like to thank everyone at the Vancouver Maritime Museum for their support in what began as an exhibit of my commercial fishing photographs and resulted in this book: specifically, Jim Delgado, Leonard McCann and Joan Thornley. Special gratitude goes to Katie Fitzgerald, Catherine Barber, Lisa Ryan and Rebecca Magellanes for their encouragement and to Susan Everts for her efforts in promoting the show. Particular appreciation goes to Dawn Hassett and Randall Graham . . . Dawn would not suffer my feigned humility during a wine fuelled conversation with Randall over the possibility of the show at the museum.

The dedication goes to Gail Blayney, my harbour for eighteen years. She gave me the time, free of commitments, to gather the images.

Then there is Alan Haig-Brown who never ceased in his enthusiastic encouragement . . . and kept me out of trouble by generously sharing his vast knowledge of the fishing industry.

When Ann West at Sono Nis gave me her darkroom last year, neither of us thought the prints for this book would emerge from it. In a world of cause and effect, much thanks goes to her generosity, and her vision for the book.

Lastly, I am *most* grateful to the crews of the boats I was welcomed aboard: *Dovre B*, *Northern Dawn*, *Snow Prince*, *Princess Colleen* and *Silver Dawn*. They fed me, gave me a bunk, and told me wonderful stories of their lives. I hope this book serves to return some measure of my appreciation, and admiration.

Brian Gauvin
May 1995

See

the boats:
canoes kayaks dingies sailing craft

Sometimes
the sea is stagnant
sometimes blowing
but no matter
at one time or another
they go or will go under

Yes
some of those I am acquainted with
have
—near the starting point
or not long after
or mid-way—
dropped below the water's skin
others pitch on
surprised to find
battered boards
remain beneath their feet

RONA MURRAY

Foreword

MORE THAN
A MERE RECORD

Fishing boats and fishing people of the world, from the little ports along the south of England to the Polynesian Islands, have long been favoured subjects of photographs. More often than not they have been used as convenient patterns for the photographer who viewed them through a camera mounted on a tripod with all three legs planted firmly on solid ground.

Only rarely has the photographer gone onboard the fishing boat to take a bunk in the fo'c's'le and to experience the close quarters, heaving decks and long hours with fishing people. To create these images, Brian Gauvin did all of this. More importantly, he has used his understanding of light and his appreciation of honest toil to create a truly fine representation of the great pride that fishing people take in their work.

The decks of a herring seiner or a halibut longliner are one of the few places in modern society where a man or woman can still experience participation in a finite crew, working directly with the elements. Life on a fishing boat is a complex of challenges governed by wind and water, tide and time, muscle and mind. The reward comes from taking on these ancient challenges and returning to port in safety and with full holds. Brian has gone onboard these boats and met the same challenges to return with countless rolls of exposed film. He has worked this film in his darkroom with all of the finesse of a master chef working with a fine fillet of halibut. He has produced graphic results that reward the eye just as the chef's culinary results reward the palate.

Brian's time on the boats also taught him the significant moments of the fishing life, and he has selected his images to represent these. The card game on the galley table while travelling to the grounds. The concentration in the baiting claim on a halibut boat as the crew prepares the gear. The concentration in the wheelhouse as the skipper focuses years of experience before committing his boat, gear and crew to setting the net. The rhythm and harmony of work on rolling decks, gaffing and swinging the halibut aboard. The tight lines and straining web around a hundred tons of herring. The harmony of the team work as crew members assemble a herring pump. Crowds of boats waiting on the ground and a pair of brothers working their big steel seiners together on a single set. The pride in the face of a young "skipper of the skiff" as he operates near the mother ship. Brian's shot of the fish gutting knives and

12 the watertight sleeves hung on the back of the cabin speaks to the utter exhaustion at the end of long days of fishing.

The photos in this book must also serve as a reminder to all of us of the thousands of years that the marine resources have provided for the people of British Columbia. They speak to us of the importance of maintaining the human values in our fisheries while safeguarding against corporate control. They tell, with great eloquence, that it is our collective responsibility to keep these images from becoming mere footnotes to west coast history.

Alan Haig-Brown
April 1995

Introduction

Cypress Bay, off the West Coast of Vancouver Island, looked like a landing site for alien space ships in March of 1988. The herring fleet, over 50 seine boats, were pumping fish into holds, the herring scales shimmering like mirror shards under glaring deck lights in the huge night. This bizarre scene was my introduction to the season opening of the herring fishery . . . a fishing life that crowds high tech equipment into remote areas with the purpose of sucking up millions of tiny fish destined for the Japanese market (where herring roe is like *gold*).

From the time I moved to Prince Rupert in 1976, I wished to photograph the fishing industry. A hint of that wish actually began in Vancouver on a miserable winter night in the early 1970s. In a bit of a funk, I was walking the Harbour Board docks when an older fellow in a plaid wool shirt invited me aboard his boat. I welcomed the company. The jug of wine he produced displayed no date and we gave it no time to age, but it improved with conversation. In the course of the conversation, he offered me a summer fishing out of Prince Rupert. I declined, but the possiblity of recording people who work on the water lodged in my consciousness.

The distance from thought to act was almost 20 years, but in 1988, Alan Haig-Brown, then editor of *Westcoast Fisherman*, chivvied me into doing a story on the herring fishery. A friend in Prince Rupert suggested I try the seiner *Northern Dawn*, so I contacted George Olafson, her skipper. He was most gracious and agreed to let me and my lenses come aboard for two weeks.

We left Steveston in March. The crew was patient with me, gentlemen in an aggressive business. The herring fishery is a huge gamble, the seine boat a very efficient vessel wrapped in a million or more dollars of licensing and sophisticated equipment. The opportunity is there to make a great deal of money in a very short time, but often the fisherman's fate is to stare at a web full of water. George, along with engineer Gordon Nichols, winchman Hans Zimmerman, skiffman Greg Olafson, second skiffman Gary Chesal, and cook/deckhand Tony Smith reflect a calmer time for fishermen. Until recently, fishing was primarily a family occupation . . . generation to generation . . . and often small scale. Now, the economics of running a high priced boat for a demanding fish company have pressed new stresses and an aggressive element into the industry.

My two weeks aboard the *Northern Dawn* were as full as two weeks can be. She was the last wooden seiner constructed at Sam Matsumoto's shipyard in North Vancouver (*circa* 1961). George Olafson, an original share owner of *Northern Dawn* had come out of retirement in 1988 to captain this trip for her new owner, Sid Smith. As we left Cypress Bay, I heard George say "The fish must have heard I retired" as he mused on the moderate 35-ton catch.

The summer saw me back in Prince Rupert aboard the *Dovre B* for a night run out to the halibut grounds in Hecate Strait. In the evening, I was shown through an opening in the wheelhouse floor to a bunk in the fo'c's'le of the old wood seiner, a nest directly above the engine. I awoke in the pitch black to the pounding engine and smell of diesel, a large swell turning my world upside down. I had no idea where I was and my stomach longed for a place to empty. I felt my way out and was about to head for the rail when I saw the crew back by the bait claim waiting for some entertainment. Pulling my stomach in and pushing my pride out, I greeted John Newton, Al Newton, Ken McDonald, John Sylvester, Mickey Pilfold and Gary Robinson. My "good morning" civility soon became truth and I was fine for the duration of the trip.

The *Dovre B* is an old wood seiner rigged for longlining halibut. "There is nothing easy about halibut," said skipper John Newton, as the work began. And so it went: hard, backbreaking work, day rolling into night and back into day five times; the crew changing positions, chopping and baiting the skate, coiling ground line, gaffing and dressing the halibut. The men would catch sleep, or a meal, one at a time, in what seemed an endless rotation. The blood and halibut slime stuck to everything and we stank in equal measure.

"I never said I'd never go halibut fishing again, but I've said lots of times I wished I was never going halibut fishing again," said John at the end of the trip. "Rupert looks better over the bow than it does over the stern," added his brother Al.

The next year, Alan, a still-on-the-hunt editor, began chasing me for another fishing story. This time we decided on a photo piece with a broader perspective than a single boat. With a brick of film, limited ideas, and even less money, I made my way to Ucluelet. Luck was mine and the first wheelhouse door I knocked on opened to a warm welcome.

Chris Cook, out of Alert Bay, handed me a cup of coffee and introduced me to the crew of *Snow Prince*: his brother Sam Cook, nephew Michael Cook, Alan Barnes, Gerry Smith and William Isaak.

We waited for the fishery to open, idling in Ucluelet for a few days and then languishing at anchor in Barkley Sound for three more. Finally, opening came; it was a day of mayhem, made more exciting for me because I was passed from boat to boat, hitchiking through the fleet.

Noise, light, smell, adrenalin—and weather, too: snow, rain, sun and rainbows. *Snow Prince* packed for *Princess Colleen*, her boat-pool partner. *Princess Colleen* had a good set, her net bulging with 150 tons of herring. Afterwards, the wheelhouse bulged as well, with the Charleston family: Con, Darryl, Joe, Patrick Jr., David, Francis and Patrick Sr.

I was aboard half a dozen boats and skiffs during the opening. A highlight was photographing on deck of the *Silver Dawn*, watching Alfred "Hutch" Hunt direct his crew, Gloria Hunt, Corrine Hunt, Ross Hunt, Tom Hunt, Dale Peeler and Robert Seyemeisder, with quiet skill through a 90-ton set.

It was a privilege to be with and photograph these people who fish for a living. Putting a frame around the chaos of a herring fishery or portraying the never-stop movement on a halibut longliner, while anticipating the actions of the crew and staying out of their way is challenging on a rocking boat. But it was absolutely exciting! As technology shifts into higher and higher gear, and as the fish become less predictable and some species disappear, there seems some importance in recording the fleet as it is now.

I focused my camera more on the people working than on boats and gear. The people are the heart of the industry—at least they were. More and more technology shapes their lives. What was once a year round activity is now, for many, a few months, for some mere weeks. Will there be a time when all there is to photograph is gear floating past unattended light stations, searching for missing fish?

Brian Gauvin
May 1995

Herring Fishing

BARKLEY SOUND
WEST COAST VANCOUVER ISLAND

—Aboard *Snow Prince, Silver Dawn* and *Princess Colleen*

Ballad of the Reluctant Fisher

18 It's not the hours of grey ocean
filling the horizon;
confusion of diesel with
blood throbbing in your ears.
It's not the days which feel like
afternoon before breakfast,
or weeks of afternoons;
evenings which promise only
the vacancy of exhaustion.
It's the hesitations between years;
remembering in winter,
yourself staring through salt-slick glass
out on the grounds;
25 sou'east, peak of the season
and no fish

Remembering the year before
yourself staring at desolate ocean
remembering winters
of anticipating summers
of foreseen moments
until dizzy with time, you move
turn from the waves, the window
and break free
already thinking of next year.

ZOË LANDALE

Then leave us free for Skeena, Ucluelet—
The time is ripe, the season's fish are running.

DOROTHY LIVESAY

It was so cold,
that night, I knew their skins were mottled like a salmon's
back: blue, white, shades of grey.

THERESA KISHKAN

Christmas at sea. The bitterest for me
That any year had given. Even so
Some had a celebration, pooled their funds
And bought the only chicken left in Alert Bay.
Others boiled cabbages in salt sea water,
Pulled out the playing cards and shrugged, and laughed.

DOROTHY LIVESAY

He is getting
a skiff ready
to go up the inlet.
He has days ahead of him,
the sea
full of herring spawn
and weed,
gathering to do
and drying.
He has a wife

seas will not bring them
together

MARILYN BOWERING

Someone has poured the sea
full; it bulges
like a dead eye,
grey on the inlet
as the lead sky's
mirror.

SÉAN VIRGO

The web is so wisely woven—wide enough to catch the biggest, fine enough to catch the smallest—that not a single thing escapes.

J. MICHAEL YATES

Listen to the sea noise,
the shudder
of the oily waves
on the fishboat's flank.

BRIAN BRETT

Sea-time has taught economy
of complaint, the futility
of curses.
Who can the men blame but
the times,
the banks, themselves?
All that weather for nothing, for years.
Sharp seas and
nausea of remorseless work;
off-shore grounds they know better
than the bodies of their wives.

ZOË LANDALE

I have looked forever
beyond Slyne Head,

have seen only waves
bullying the fisherman,
have seen only a horizon
too far away for sailing.

THERESA KISHKAN

              We have been here
before, eating raw air, but have always
forgotten,

all day eating the air the light
impales,
         stalking the singular animal.

   I no longer remember whether a fish
or a bird.   Nor whether its song or its silence
is what we were listening for.

ROBERT BRINGHURST

With claw fingers
  combing out
Darklands of water weed
From the morning nets,
  they remember . . .

SÉAN VIRGO

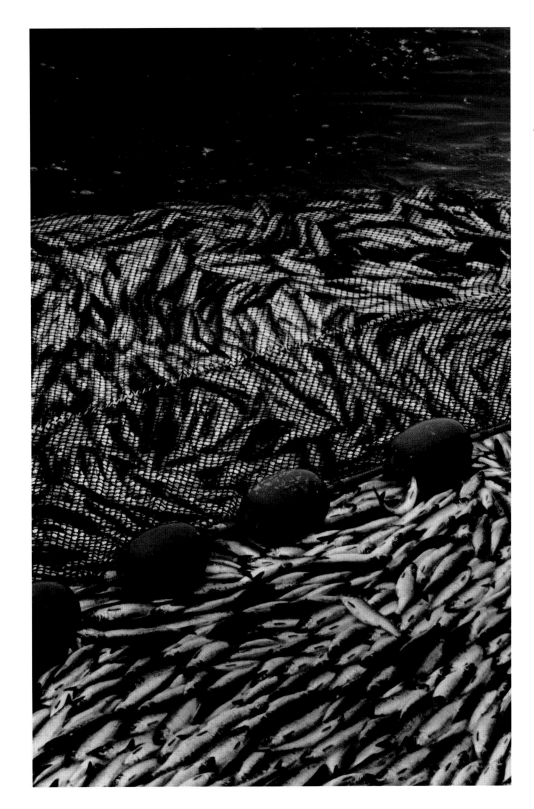

Mountains dazzling in the sun,
The Skeena, wide here, below the dazzle,
Catching the shapes, the snow twice;
The railway along the edge, the road
To the ocean, the coast of timber and salmon

RALPH GUSTAFSON

Here no harbour ever was;
no children wander barefoot
dragging their forked sticks
   in the sand;
no castles dare
   the water's edge;
nor do men find rest
   from their long days
hauling and heaving
   the nets—

ANN YORK

Out of the wordless innocence of the sea
they came, leaving the pure
movement of shark, ray, squid
behind, the bright slice through oblivious
waters that being alive
had meant, the never ending
to-fro tug, asleep or dead, of ocean

JAMES HARRISON

a light like the sea's
interspersed with gulls and terns
suspended between two winds,
the wind from hereafter,
the wind from the land

HAROLD ENRICO

The dark weight of a
night's haul within them,
the old men turned east and
cast to an offered shore.
Trailed from her thin grey wake
into morning, she was riding
the last wave out.

SUSAN MUSGRAVE

The skipper on the seiner *Colleen Nicole*
has a sense of humour
A fish twists from the seiner's forestay
cloth indigo   swimming in air
Sometimes I see a woman dancing
long skirts divided, wind extending arms
hooked, desperate

ZOË LANDALE

If there is nothing,
I know, still,
    an animal is swimming
Toward me
    through dark water,
Through dark wetness
Without sense
Of malice
Or of kill.

J. MICHAEL YATES

Halibut Longlining

HECATE STRAIT
QUEEN CHARLOTTE ISLANDS

—Aboard *Dovre B*

Lines from the Log

42   There are beaches below Estevan
where the coast splays out;
how white the seabirds there
above the chilled blue, how pale the wind
among the gulls
and everything a soft cry.

Beyond the islands
more islands, then the flooding ocean stream:
Chinese, Russian, Japanese—
more the boundaries of dream than navigation.
My charts cannot follow the albatross,
or the flight of those longwinged
deepchested wanderers coming and going
in stories men tell who've been back
from as far as they can go,
and lounge on deck watching seacrows belly
into Hecate's pallid swelling.

Along tortuous inland channels
the spray fragrant as lilac
where words invent the past,
more words the future.
Here history simplifies nothing
and love betrays us all.

CHARLES LILLARD

44

I cry arrogance:
That hurl of the god
Is my hurl,
Against death,
Hard, flung, swift as
The target of trident
Slipped in the moving, great
Dark of the motionless wave.

RALPH GUSTAFSON

for those who are born
    between sun and moon
have no fear of
    their lawful tides,
they move with
    their own sea ways
and the great waters
    will not engulf them.

GWLADYS DOWNES

Decks trust my feet.
  I go below. Brown ribs
curve around me. I am
  beating like its heart
and crouch a moment, carving bone,
  hunched, patient.
Gulls cry out like
  children high above.
Seas roar like streets.
  We are the last to leave
in hurrying rain.

ROBIN SKELTON

48

The things we set forth after
Over dark water.
Light line. Hostile weather.

J. MICHAEL YATES

I am ringed in
with deep black water
and the shell-stink of tides.

I am alone with the rush of my blood.

It is dark out—
The sky is matted with fog.

I listen with a beating ear.

HAROLD RHENISCH

Men at dawn will be fishermen,
half bear, part heron,
as their fingers troll the river,
like an ouzel's dark hesitation

CHARLES LILLARD

I would lose what I never had:
Certain fish: uncertain fate. I know
Where I am by where I have been.

J. MICHAEL YATES

. . . I stepped outside
and the wind bolted
down my neck,

I came to myself easily:
sunlight—we didn't really know
it when we had it—
is gone and rain is a bad joke,

HAROLD RHENISCH

Ahead of us the sea's swelling purple;
astern, the fish scow, our jobs
and all the work piling up
like off-loaded cargo.

CHARLES LILLARD

Herring Fishing

CYPRESS BAY, TOFINO
VANCOUVER ISLAND

—Aboard Northern Dawn

More Than Halfway There

56 I am
at this moment
somewhere beyond
the middle of
the journey

you ahead
you and you behind

But our charts
appear to be
quite incomplete
with information
missing from the start

We have to guess
            rely on omens
                    or messages we think we find
                    but cannot understand

We check the map:
            one side up
            then another

            Directions it contains
            could point to north or south
                            west or east
            do not indicate
            the cost incurred
            if we have wandered off

                        the route

RONA MURRAY

The wolves say to the dogs what the madman of me says to the citizen. I need to go fishing until I need to return.

J. MICHAEL YATES

Wrapping up our ocean elegies
In thunderous jests, turning deaf ears
To the hobnob silence of empty shores;
Try our luck—

RALPH GUSTAFSON

From a fisherwoman
I learned this knitting
of life and home into a net
that her fisherman would live in,
while out riding the crazy sea.

MARNIE DUFF

The rising mist,
Rising above
The Skeena, Fraser, Nass,
Rising from pine shadows,
Rising from a height of land
    At Raven's lair;
The Skeena, Fraser, Nass,
The Dean, Bella Coola, Sombrio,
Flooding the Pacific's maw . . .

CHARLES LILLARD

Three days out
and a level sea unwinding
the spools of a white wake,
no birds attendant
yet . . .

ROBIN SKELTON

How can you tell
it will rain, when the sun
lies still on the salt glitter?
clouds move dark-rose and grey
with small whales trailing after

GWLADYS DOWNES

I wait out the night,
listening into my empty miles
for my mind to break, rubbing
the loose touch
of wind gently
into my skin.

HAROLD RHENISCH

Fish that neither floats
nor sinks but holds its own
effortlessly as a burnished

swirl, midstream, around
some sunken rock, water
sluicing through its gills

and along flanks that adjust
ceaselessly to a shifting
flow—fish that emerges

from and melts back into
ubiquity like a half
recaptured memory.
                    Fish.

JAMES HARRISON

I never knew him
but with lurking eyes
had watched from the
summerhouse
his deep-water body
that moved like a fish
inviting the lure.

SUSAN MUSGRAVE

At the Dock

STEVESTON, PRINCE RUPERT
VANCOUVER

The Casual Assurance of Limbs

72
When I was a fisher,
safe   upon the certainty
of sea,
horizons were owned with
the casual assurance of limbs;
landmarks pulled   litheness of muscles;
diesel   with co-ordination.
Meals were cluttered with
cloud formations,
waves were recurrences
which probed through dreams like
long streamers   of kelp.

Everyone lied.
Between the weatherman and dockside bragging
sometimes it seemed
that only the fish, with their
protesting gape of death,
had anything at all to say.

There were balances
Beneath the second skin of planking,
cared for more tenderly than flesh,
dark miles of water
spread arms   across the world.

ZOË LANDALE

Fish aren't designed
 as dissociated
observers of what they do.
 For them, life
is what they throw themselves
 into in one long shudder,
the whole body
 a total act of murder.

JAMES HARRISON

If this were a story I'd end it now. There are no more voices to shout from the sea . . .

THERESA KISHKAN

Poetry Sources

GEORGE AMABILE: p. 79. From "Inner Space: The Light Culture" *Blood Ties*, SNP 1972

MARILYN BOWERING: p. 24. From "North Coast Lament" *The Killing Room*, SNP 1977

BRIAN BRETT: p. 27. From "Fishboat and Dreamer" *Poems New and Selected*, SNP 1993

ROBERT BRINGHURST: p. 30. From "Ararat" *Bergschrund*, SNP 1975

GWLADYS DOWNES: pp. 45, 64. From "Swimmer," "Seals" *Out of the Violent Dark*, SNP 1978

MARNIE DUFF: p. 60. From "Knitting Myself" *Caught Soul*, SNP 1987

HAROLD ENRICO: p. 35. From "The Desert and After: La Terra Promessa" *Now, A Thousand Years From Now*, SNP 1975

RALPH GUSTAFSON: pp. 32, 44, 59. From "In The Coast Range," "Of Death-Dealing Poseidon," "On This Sea-Floor" *Collected Poems*, Vol. I, SNP 1987

JAMES HARRISON: pp. 34, 67, 75. From "Islands" *Flying Dutchmen*, SNP 1983

THERESA KISHKAN: pp. 29; 21, 76. From "Inishturbot" *Six Poets of B.C.*, SNP 1980; "Everything in its Grave" *Ikons of the Hunt*, SNP 1978

ZOË LANDALE: pp. 18, 28, 38, 72. From "Ballad of the Reluctant Fisher," "The Myth of the Self-Made Man," "The Colour of Winter Air," "The Casual Assurance of Limbs" *Colour of Winter Air*, SNP 1990

CHARLES LILLARD: pp. 42, 50, 53; 62. From "Lines From The Log," "Kolosh Ryeka," "Moving into the Territory" *A Coastal Range*, SNP 1984; "Rivers Were Promises" *Voice My Shaman*, SNP 1976

78   DOROTHY LIVESAY: pp. 19, 23. From "Call My People Home" *The Self-Completing Tree*, PRESS PORCEPIC 1986

RONA MURRAY: pp. 10, 56. From "Stassis," "More Than Halfway There" *Journey*, SNP 1981

SUSAN MUSGRAVE: pp. 36, 68. From "The Tribe of the Sea," "Requiem" *Selected Strawberries & Other Poems*, SNP 1977

HAROLD RHENISCH: pp. 52; 49, 66. From "Becher Bay" *A Delicate Fire*, SNP 1989; "Island," "Open Letter" *Winter*, SNP 1982

ROBIN SKELTON: pp. 47; 63. From "New Bedford" *Collected Shorter Poems*, SNP 1981; "Voyage" *Collected Longer Poems*, SNP 1985

SÉAN VIRGO: pp. 31; 25. From "Net Hags" *Pieces For The Old Earth Man*, SNP 1973; "Grey" *Deathwatch on Skidigate Narrows*, SNP 1979

J. MICHAEL YATES: pp. 39, 48, 51, 57; 26; 6. From "Transparency of Blackness," "Death the Second," "Canto Six," "Long Light" (GBLM) *Nothing Speaks for the Blue Moraines*, SNP 1973; "Timesmiths in Space" *Breath of the Snow Leopard*, SNP 1974; "The Net" *Quarks*, PLAYWRIGHTS CO-OP 1975

ANN YORK: p. 33. From "Era Beach" *Agapanthus*, SNP 1987

Off the coast
the gill nets fan open from their creaking drums
like the wings of insects
between the leadline
and the string of puffed rice corks

Suspended in seawater
they're invisible
Keeping them straight in a running tide
takes more than patience
& less than the rack
of charts collecting dust on the cabin ceiling

All afternoon
the voices of other fishermen
not saying much
crackle
around a loose connection

GEORGE AMABILE

Gill net fishing is not shown in any of the photographs in this book.

Gone Fishing

DISPLAY AND TEXT TYPE
SET IN CASLON.
PHOTOGRAPHS ARE DUO-TONES
PRINTED OFFSET ON
EIGHTY POUND
DULL COATED PAPER